The NFL's Greatest Teams

New York Jets

Marcia Zappa

Big Buddy Books
An Imprint of Abdo Publishing
www.abdopublishing.com

www.abdopublishing.com

Published by Abdo Publishing, a division of ABDO, PO Box 398166, Minneapolis, Minnesota 55439.
Copyright © 2015 by Abdo Consulting Group, Inc. International copyrights reserved in all countries. No part
of this book may be reproduced in any form without written permission from the publisher. Big Buddy Books™
is a trademark and logo of Abdo Publishing.

Printed in the United States of America, North Mankato, Minnesota.
092014
012015

Cover Photo: ASSOCIATED PRESS.
Interior Photos: ASSOCIATED PRESS (pp. 5, 7, 9, 13, 14, 15, 16, 17, 18, 19, 20, 21, 23, 25, 27, 29); Diamond
        Images/Getty Images (p. 11); Getty Images (p. 28).

Coordinating Series Editor: Rochelle Baltzer
Contributing Editors: Megan M. Gunderson, Sarah Tieck
Graphic Design: Michelle Labatt

Library of Congress Cataloging-in-Publication Data

Zappa, Marcia, 1985-
  New York Jets / Marcia Zappa.
      pages cm. -- (The NFL's Greatest Teams)
  Audience: Age: 7-11.
  ISBN 978-1-62403-589-0
1. New York Jets (Football team)--History--Juvenile literature. I. Title.
  GV956.N37Z37 2015
  796.332'64097471--dc23
                              2014026442

Contents

A Winning Team

The New York Jets are a football team in the National Football League (NFL). They are based in Florham Park, New Jersey. But, they are a home team for New York City, New York.

The Jets have had good seasons and bad. But time and again, they've proven themselves. Let's see what makes the Jets one of the NFL's greatest teams.

Green and white are the team's colors.

5

League Play

Team Standings

The AFC and the National Football Conference (NFC) make up the NFL. Each conference has a north, south, east, and west division.

The NFL got its start in 1920. Its teams have changed over the years. Today, there are 32 teams. They make up two conferences and eight divisions.

The Jets play in the East Division of the American Football Conference (AFC). This division also includes the Buffalo Bills, the Miami Dolphins, and the New England Patriots.

The Patriots (*above*) and the Dolphins are longtime rivals of the Jets.

Fans get excited to watch their team play rivals.

Kicking Off

The Jets started play in 1960. They were one of the first teams in the American Football League (AFL). At first, the team was called the Titans. Their colors were gold and blue.

New York City already had a **professional** football team called the New York Giants. This made it hard for the Titans to gain fans and sell tickets.

The team played three seasons as the Titans.

Early star players included wide receiver Don Maynard.

Highlight Reel

Win or Go Home

NFL teams play 16 regular season games each year. The teams with the best records are part of the play-off games. Play-off winners move on to the conference championships. Then, conference winners face off in the Super Bowl!

In 1963, new owners bought the Titans. They changed the team's name and colors to what they are today. And, they hired head coach Weeb Ewbank.

In 1965, quarterback Joe Namath joined the Jets. In 1967, the Jets had their first winning season. The next year, they made it to the play-offs. They went on to the Super Bowl! They beat the Baltimore Colts 16–7.

Many people were surprised when the Jets won the 1969 Super Bowl. They expected the Colts to win.

In 1970, the AFL joined the NFL. The Jets didn't make it back to the play-offs until 1981. They were successful off and on for the rest of the 1980s and 1990s. They went to the play-offs five times.

The Jets began to make the play-offs regularly during the 2000s. They played in the AFC **championship** in 2010 and 2011. But, they didn't make it back to the Super Bowl.

In 2010, the Jets lost to the Indianapolis Colts 30–17 in the AFC championship.

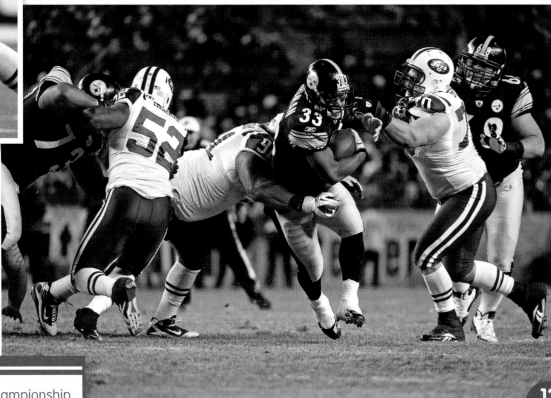

In 2011, the Jets lost the AFC championship to the Pittsburgh Steelers 24–19.

Halftime! Stat Break

Team Records

RUSHING YARDS
Career: Curtis Martin, 10,302 yards (1998–2005)
Single Season: Curtis Martin, 1,697 yards (2004)
PASSING YARDS
Career: Joe Namath, 27,057 yards (1965–1976)
Single Season: Joe Namath, 4,007 yards (1967)
RECEPTIONS
Career: Don Maynard, 627 receptions (1960–1972)
Single Season: Al Toon, 93 receptions (1988)
ALL-TIME LEADING SCORER
Pat Leahy, 1,470 points, (1974–1991)

Famous Coaches

Weeb Ewbank (1963–1973)

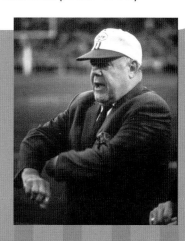

Championships

SUPER BOWL APPEARANCES:	SUPER BOWL WINS:
1969	1969

Pro Football Hall of Famers & Their Years with the Jets

Weeb Ewbank, Coach (1963–1973)
Curtis Martin, Running Back (1998–2005)
Don Maynard, Wide Receiver (1960–1972)
Joe Namath, Quarterback (1965–1976)
John Riggins, Running Back (1971–1975)

Fan Fun

NICKNAME: Gang Green
STADIUM: MetLife Stadium
LOCATION: East Rutherford, New Jersey

Coaches' Corner

Weeb Ewbank was already a successful NFL coach when he took over the Jets in 1963. He turned the struggling team around. He led the Jets to win their first Super Bowl in 1969!

Rex Ryan began coaching the Jets in 2009.

Ewbank led the team to more wins than any other Jets coach.

Star Players

Don Maynard WIDE RECEIVER (1960–1972)

Don Maynard was the first player to sign with the New York Titans. He was always a strong player. But, it wasn't until he teamed up with quarterback Joe Namath that he really began to shine. During his time with the Jets, Maynard had 627 receptions. That is a team record.

Joe Namath QUARTERBACK (1965–1976)

Joe Namath quickly became a star. He was known for being flashy. So, he was often called "Broadway Joe." Namath led the team to its only Super Bowl win. He was named the game's Most Valuable Player (MVP). When Namath **retired**, he had passed for 27,057 yards. That is more than any other Jet.

Joe Klecko DEFENSIVE LINEMAN (1977–1987)

Joe Klecko was chosen late in the 1977 **draft**. He became an important part of the team's defensive line. During his **career**, Klecko played defensive end, defensive tackle, and nose tackle. He is one of the only NFL players to play in the Pro Bowl, which is the league's all-star game, at three different positions.

Wesley Walker WIDE RECEIVER (1977–1989)

Wesley Walker played for the Jets his whole **career**. Even though he only had one healthy eye, Walker was a star receiver. Over the years, he had 438 receptions and 71 touchdowns. He helped the team make it to the play-offs several times in the 1980s.

Mark Gastineau DEFENSIVE END (1979–1988)

Mark Gastineau was known for his skill rushing the quarterback. In 1984, he had 22 sacks. This was a league record for many years. When he **retired**, Gastineau had 107.5 sacks. That is more than any other Jet.

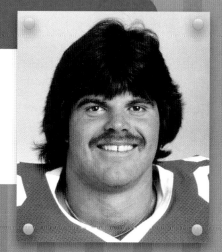

Freeman McNeil RUNNING BACK (1981–1992)

Freeman McNeil was the team's first pick in the 1981 **draft**. He was the third pick overall. In 1982, Freeman became the first Jet to lead the NFL in rushing yards. When he **retired**, McNeil had 8,074 rushing yards. That was a team record for many years.

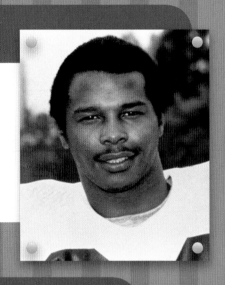

Curtis Martin RUNNING BACK (1998–2005)

Curtis Martin joined the Jets in 1998. He rushed for more than 1,000 yards during every season he played for the team except one. In all, he rushed for 10,302 yards as a Jet. That is a team record.

MetLife Stadium

The New York Jets play home games at MetLife Stadium. It is in East Rutherford, New Jersey. MetLife Stadium opened in 2010. It can hold about 82,500 people. The New York Giants also play home games there.

East Rutherford is near New York City. But, it has more space for a large stadium.

Go Gang Green!

Thousands of fans go to MetLife Stadium to see the Jets play home games. Some fans call their team "Gang Green." Others **chant** "J-E-T-S, Jets! Jets! Jets!" And sometimes, fireworks explode around the stadium.

In 2013, a drum line called the Aviators started playing at home games. They play each time the Jets score a touchdown.

Fans enjoy local favorite foods at home games. This includes meatballs (*left*), pork rolls, and pepper and egg sandwiches.

Final Call

The Jets have a long, rich history. They were Super Bowl **champions** in 1969.

Even during losing seasons, true fans have stuck by them. Many believe the New York Jets will remain one of the greatest teams in the NFL.

Jets fans love getting to meet players.

Through the Years

1960

The team plays its first season as part of the AFL. They are called the Titans.

1963

The team's name changes to the Jets.

1967

The Jets have their first winning season.

1970

The AFL joins the NFL.

1969

The Jets win the Super Bowl! They beat the Baltimore Colts 16–7.

28

2008

The Jets beat the Saint Louis Rams 47–3. This is the biggest win in team history.

2010

MetLife Stadium opens.

1981

The Jets make it to the play-offs for the first time since 1969.

1978

Coach Weeb Ewbank becomes the first Jet in the Pro Football Hall of Fame.

2013

Geno Smith sets a team record. He is the first Jets **rookie** quarterback to pass for more than 300 yards in a game.

Postgame Recap

1. What was the original team name of the Jets?
   A. The Giants **B**. The Airplanes **C**. The Titans

2. What is the name of the stadium where the Jets play home games?
   A. MetLife Stadium **B**. Jets Stadium **C**. Shea Stadium

3. Where is the stadium located?
   A. New York City, New York
   B. Florham Park, New Jersey
   C. East Rutherford, New Jersey

4. Name 2 of the 5 Jets in the Pro Football Hall of Fame.

5. Why was Joe Namath called "Broadway Joe"?
   A. He could throw across a crowded field.
   B. He grew up near Broadway in New York City.
   C. He was flashy.

1. C. 2. A. 3. C. 4. See page 15 5. C.

Glossary

career a period of time spent in a certain job.

champion the winner of a championship, which is a game, a match, or a race held to find a first-place winner.

chant to repeat a word or a phrase to a beat. Usually, chants are spoken loudly by a crowd.

draft a system for professional sports teams to choose new players. When a team drafts a player, they choose that player for their team.

professional (pruh-FEHSH-nuhl) paid to do a sport or activity.

retire to give up one's job.

rookie a first-year player in a professional sport.

Websites

To learn more about the NFL's Greatest Teams, visit **booklinks.abdopublishing.com**. These links are routinely monitored and updated to provide the most current information available.

Index